TIN
CRAFT

A Work Book by
FERN-RAE ABRAHAM

SUNSTONE
PRESS

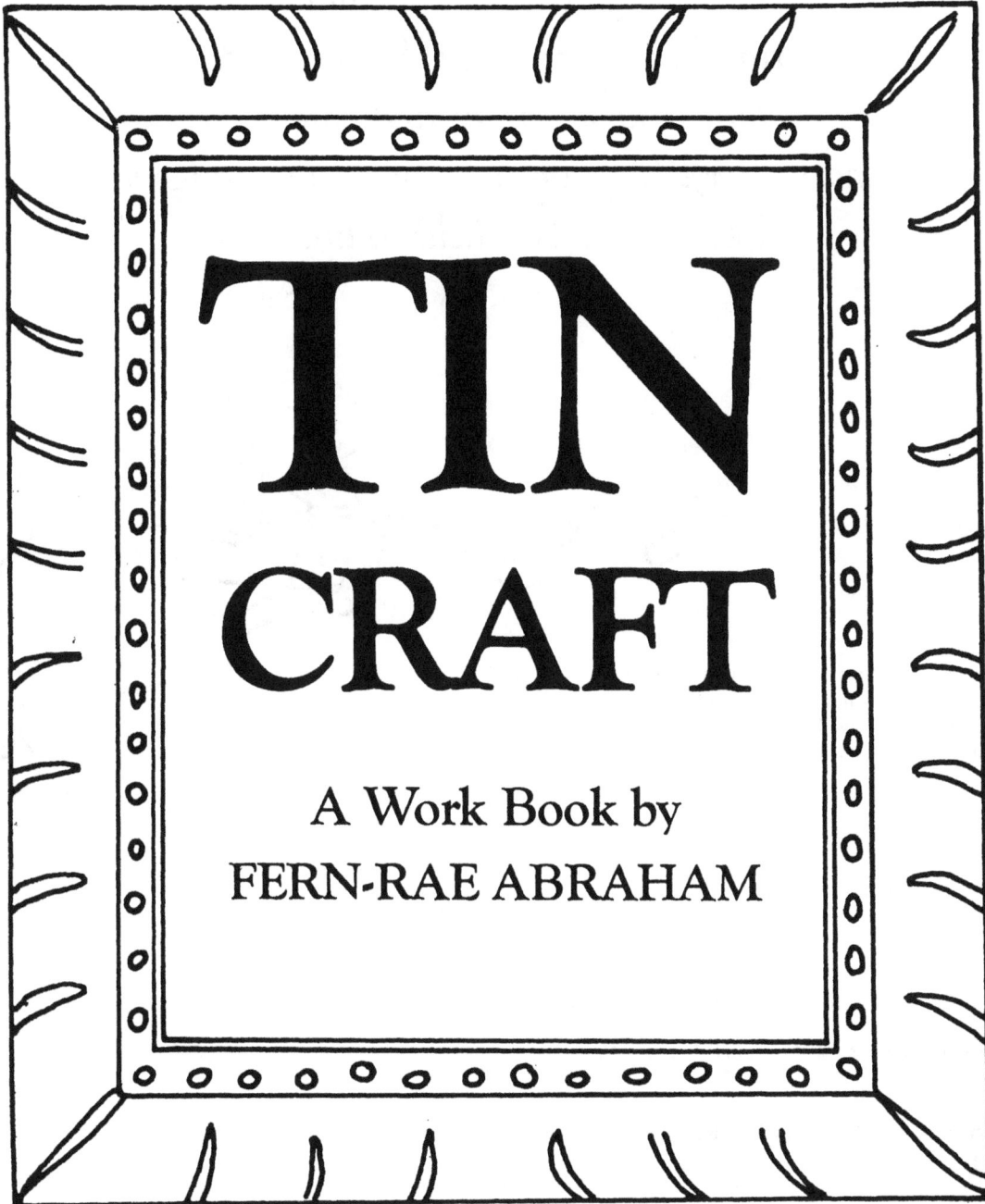

SANTA FE
NEW MEXICO

TINCRAFT
2

To my Mom, who taught a little child:
"Beautiful hands are those that do work
that is noble, brave and true,"
and to Beryl Boynton, who of all the craftsmen
I ever knew best held to this ideal.

–F.R.A.

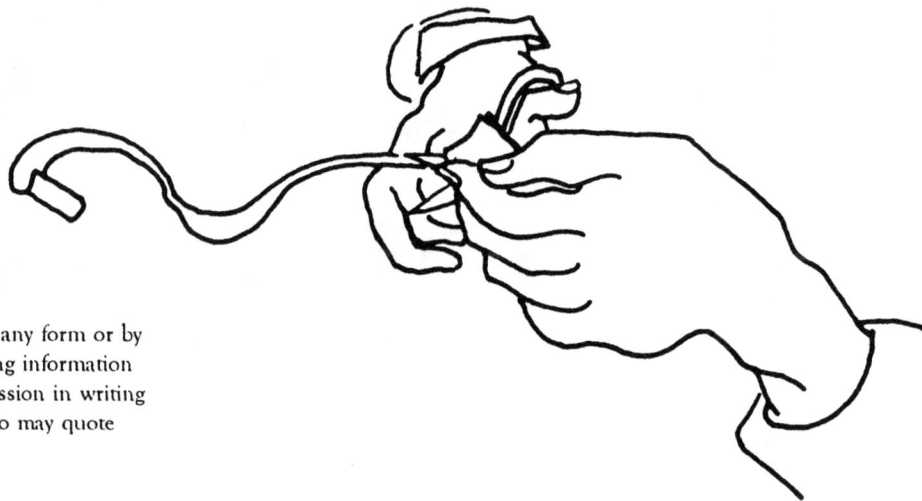

Revised edition

Printed in the United States of America

Library of Congress Cataloging-in-Publication Data

Abraham, Fern-Rae. 1912-
    Tin craft : a work book / by Fern-Rae Abraham. – Rev. ed.
        p. cm.
    Includes bibliographical references.
    ISBN: 0-86534-098-6
    1. Tinsmithing. 2. Tin cans. 3. Decoration and ornament-
Plant forms. I. Title.
TT266.A268 1994
739.5'32–dc20   93-46615
                                            CIP

Published by Sunstone Press
        Post Office Box 2321
        Santa Fe, New Mexico 87504-2321 / USA
        (505) 988-4418 / FAX: (505) 988-1025
        orders only (800) 243-5644

FLOWER SPRAY WITH BIRDS
See Project No. 2 and Project No. 8

TABLE OF CONTENTS

INTRODUCTION

In the winter of 1950 sculptors Beryl Boynton and her husband Ray, a retired art professor formerly of the University of California at Berkeley, set out on a painting trip into the spectacular Texas Big Bend National Park along the Mexican Border.

As always, while Ray sketched and painted, Beryl longed for something to occupy her talents. Her hammered copper and brass relief sculpture was well known on the West Coast, and now she more and more wished to work with a kindred medium.

It would have to be portable, she thought, and simple to obtain, plentiful and inexpensive, for although they had enough retirement money to live on and to buy a reasonable amount of art supplies, the high cost of brass, copper or silver sheets made the use of these particular metals out-of-the-question. Yet — the medium had to be metal!

Then one day, looking for a spot to start sketching, they came to a little graveyard. Ray, for no apparent reason, stopped the car, and they got out to stand in this quiet place where the stillness was broken only by the blowing wind.

The usual few wooden crosses stood at odd angles in the hard earth. Dates scratched on them marked them as very old. In a state of complete neglect, long forgotten, the wind's constant passage had almost obliterated the spot; yet Beryl felt there was something in this forlorn place trying to speak to them.

Then they saw the delicate ornaments. There was one on nearly every cross, or half-buried in the hard, wind-swept ground. Perhaps only these two artists would have noticed these rust-encrusted objects with more than a curious glance. Ray and Beryl began to examine them.

At first it was simply odd and interesting to find ornaments in that out-of-the-way place. Their excitement grew, because the tin, as it appeared to be, was weathered and oxidized into an amazing beauty by years of sun, wind, blowing sand and sparse rain. Against the gray of the wooden crosses and dry earth, the rusted shades of red and brown, even purple and black, created a rich and varied texture.

They discovered several designs: wreaths, baskets, birds and sprays of flowers. The pieces were scalloped and fringed with scissors, then bent, twisted, looped and shaped by hand, and fastened together with wires. Nothing so sophisticated as solder had been used. Holes for the wires had been punched with nails or a knife.

"Purely out of love and necessity!" thought Beryl.

Looking around where the desert stretched to the horizon, she guessed there had been little water to grow a living flower, yet in their loving and caring these people had been given inspiration and found a way to create beauty.

Beryl was positive that the flowers had been made from tin cans, for she could see the pressed rings of the manufactured lids in the petals. As she stood there she saw the solution to her problem and from it worked out her own tin craft.

One thing that surprised and delighted Beryl when she began to experiment with her first tin — something she had hardly noticed before — was that the cans are lined with a gold lacquer that can be used in contrast to the silver tones.

Soon she began making patterns from living flowers to make her designs. Later she tried ways of tooling the metal to make the pieces more interesting and realistic. To add charm and color she used "jewels" in the centers of flowers and for bird's eyes.

After Beryl had taught me to work with the tin, I felt that a book should be made to preserve this craft and make it available to others. Beryl was happy to help me in any way possible. I have tried to present it in a practical working form, more as a springboard to further creativity than as a cut-and-dried method for copying.

I might point out that since tin is a stubborn material, and cutting the tin creates sharp edges, it is not a suitable medium for small children to handle. However many of the projects could be made out of stout paper or cardboard, with the use of proper adhesives or staples fastening parts together.

All these designs were made for tin, keeping in mind the unique character of tin, it's springiness, availability, color, brightness, and the speed and ease with which it can be joined, soldered and cleaned. It should also be noted that aluminum or aluminum cans are not suitable for this work. Aluminum cannot, for instance, be soldered with the easily available, ordinary and inexpensive type of solder that a craftsman can use on tin.

When I met Beryl Boynton she had been working with tin for several years and had become quite adept at it. She had sold pieces almost from the start, and had taught a few students to do the work. It is my desire and hope that many other craftsmen will now enjoy working with this interesting and challenging craft.

—FERN-RAE ABRAHAM

TIN WREATH
Made of gold and silver tin can material. Bird has jewelled eye, and two flowers have jewelled centers.

MATERIALS

TIN CANS

Tin cans of all sizes, shapes and types, while not as plentiful as they once were, are still available and are your first and most important material in TIN CRAFT. The metal used to make the cans combines steel and tin, a thin sheet of steel sandwiched between two very thin sheets of pure tin. Cans are recorded to amount to about ninety-eight percent steel and two percent tin. The cost, for our purpose, depends largely on your ingenuity in procuring, and saving, cans and lids made from tin.

For leaves and other flat pieces you will need the sides of No. 2 and No. 3 cans, while larger projects, such as wall murals, the angel, swag and others, will need large fruit and syrup tins. You can ask at a favorite restaurant if these large cans are still made from tin. Some of the fruit tins have the brightest lining colors — as you will discover when you begin your collection.

LIDS

Can lids, since they are round to begin with, save a great deal of labor in cutting. Another advantage is that no sheet of tin that you buy is coated with gold-colored, fired-on lacquer used by the manufacturers to coat the insides of fruit, meat and vegetable tins. This coating prevents discoloration or bleaching of foods preserved in the cans, but for the worker in tin, it is strictly an ornamental bonus.

WIRE

Galvanized wire in three sizes is used throughout this book — 16, 18 and 22 gauge. Fine iron binding wire that will not take solder is helpful to have for tying pieces together while soldering. After the solder is hardened, the binding wire is unwound and taken off. Although binding wire is good to know about, it is not a necessity as there are a number of ways to hold pieces together. These will be described later. All gauges of wire can be bought in hardware and hobby shops.

The heaviest wire, 16 gauge, is used for stems, for the circle that is the base of the wreath, and for any projects that take a sturdy wire. Coat hanger wire is too rigid, unless you decide to make something larger and heavier than anything in this book.

Medium-size, 18 gauge wire is used for smaller stems and more delicate work, as indicated in each separate piece diagrammed in the book. The finest wire, 22 gauge is most important for binding flowers and leaves onto stems. This binding is done as tightly as possible and is permanently soldered into the piece. It is distinguished from the "binding wire" mentioned above which is removed after soldering.

JEWELS

"Jewels" add the finishing touch to a beautiful piece of work. Look for glittery colorful buttons for your first pieces. Buttons are easy to fasten on, simply by running a fine wire (binding wire, 22 gauge is good for this) through the loop or holes of the button and wiring it into place. Also try gluing them on with household or epoxy-type glues if you can get buttons with flat backs. If not, you can cut them off so they are flat.

There is one thing to think of when buying buttons or jewelry to use on your tin pieces — is it possible to fasten the pieces on? All kinds of costume jewelry can be used, as mentioned, if you can find a way to fasten it on.

TOOLS

Can Opener: This should be a strong, wall-type opener, either manual or electric

Two Hammers: Ball peen, and 13 ounce ordinary hammer.

Pruning Shears or Poultry Shears: I use a pair of Wiss pruning shears, 8 inches long, with the cutting end only 2¼ inches long. Hardware stores sell them.

Old Flat Iron, Piece of Railroad Track or other heavy iron: This is used for an anvil, a weight and a resting place for the soldering iron.

Awl or Nail: For punching holes. This can also be used a a stylus to scratch lines and draw around patterns before cutting tin.

Files: Carpenter's flat files, or the long three cornered files are very good for filing off sharp edges and slivers of tin after cutting.

Soldering Iron: This can be of medium weight, an inexpensive electric iron of either the stick or gun type.

Acid Core Solder: Hardware or variety stores sell this on spools.

Long-nosed Pliers with Built-in wire cutter: For turning and curling wire or tin.

Punches for Tooling (several sizes): You will need a blunt, round-point, enough to make a dapple, but not sharp enough to punch a hole.

Cold Chisel or similar instrument: For tooling lines in tin. I use a heavy old knife.

Small Dustpan and a Whisk Broom or Four-Inch Stuff Brush: For sweeping up tin scraps after each work session.

Tin Snips with Spring: The spring makes it easier on hands.

Sandpaper: For removing rust and dulling sharp edges.

Clamps: For securing pieces whil soldering.

TOOLS AND MATERIALS FOR DESIGNING

ruler	erasers	tracing paper
triangle	compass	sketch paper
medium-hard "HB" pencils	carbon paper	cardboard

LONG HANDLED BRUSH

SMALL DUST PAN

WIRE

TIN CANS

TOOLS

CAN OPENER

WISS PRUNING

RUBBER

MALLET

POULTRY SHEARS

WHISK BROOM

SHEARS WITH SPRING

WASTE BASKET

BALL PEEN

HAMMER

MAIL ORDER CATALOG OR SLICK MAGAZINE

PLIERS

NAIL AWL

COLD CHISEL

FILES

SOLDERING IRON

SOLDER

FLATIRON

SAND PAPER

RULER

YARD STICK

PREPARATION

The first requirement in preparing the tin, of course, is to clean the cans. My method is to routinely wash and dry all cans in the kitchen. I remove the paper wrappers while they are still wet. The cans are then carried into the studio to a large wooden box. Lids are stored in a smaller box.

[Note: We don't remove the bottoms of the cans while they are in the kitchen because we use cans for mixing paint as well as for many other purposes. This way the whole family knows where to get a clean tin can at any time, and the bottoms are only removed as a new tin project is planned.]

When the tops and bottoms have been removed, cut out the side seams with your shears. This requires care; the tin is stiff and it is easy to cut yourself. As soon as the seam has beem cut off, take a medium-to-coarse piece of flint sandpaper and sand carefully, dulling all the sharp edges. Take care not to scratch the lacquered sides of the tin.

If there is any glue on the side where the label was fastened on, remove it by scraping gently with a dull knife or wooden straightedge. Again, try not to scratch through the thin coating.

Now gently rub the curve out of the can. By bending it slightly into an opposite curve, it will sping back almost flat. It it doesn't, repeat the process until it does, but don't bend any sharp angles into it.

Nothing has to be done to perpare the lids after they have been washed and dried. "Lids," of course, refers to both tops and bottoms of cans.

PREPARING CANS FOR USE:

A: Remove bottom of can.

B. Remove bottom and top rims.

C. Remove seam.

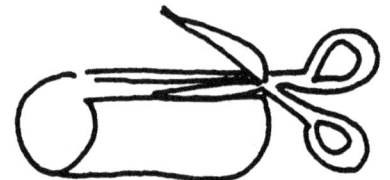

D. Bend can straight across knee. Rub gently to flatten tin.

SOLDERING

Soldering, for the purposes outlined here – the process of joining two pieces of tin – is simple. A soft solder is used in the simplest manner and should be no source of worry, even if you have never before soldered anything.

A medium weight electric soldering iron is necessary, either rod or gun type, and a supply of acid-core solder. Adequate instructions come with the iron.

After "tinning" the iron tip (the package directions will explain the process), the next step is to be sure that all surfaces to be soldered are clean. If there is any doubt, wash the tin with a brush in hot soap or detergent bath, rinse well and dry in a warm place. The soldering will be easier if the piece is warm.

The two pieces to be soldered together must fit flatly against each other and must be held steadily. Here is the place to use the binding wire if you have it. However, your own ingenuity and resourcefulness will be called into play to find the best method for applying the solder. You may have to use weights, clamps, wire, string or whatever will do the job.

Now, for the actual soldering job, uncoil several inches of the solder from the spool, but don't cut it off. Hold the spool in one hand and the soldering iron in the other. Be sure the iron has been pre-heated enough so it will melt the solder when touched to it. The iron should rest for a few seconds on the tin to warm up the spot to be soldered; then, touch the tip end of solder down on the joint as closely as possible to the tip of the iron, or even directly on the iron.

The solder will melt immediately and run down into the joint. Remove the iron and the solder, being careful not to shift or move the tin. Wait a second or two to allow it to cool and harden, and the job is done. Now you can remove the clamps (or whatever you have used to hold the pieces together) and proceed to the next spot that has to be soldered.

If it doesn't hold, it will be because the tin isn't clean or it doesn't have a flat, tight joint. Perhaps the pieces shifted before the solder had time to cool. Scrape the solder off, wash again, and give it another try. Experience will teach you to make a neat job.

Having used acid-core solder, as soon as you finish a piece, you will have to wash it in a detergent bath of ammonia and water. A large pan, sink or bathtub is best because the whole article should be under the water. Scrub each soldered spot with a stiff brush and plenty of suds. I use a long-handled one or two-inch brush which saves the hands from contact with the sharp edges of the tin. Washing is necessary to remove the acid which will continue to act and would soon discolor and rust the work. Wash your hands frequently while working.

Electric Soldering Iron

solder

Heat up and "tin" new Iron before using

soldering a wreath

Asbestos or metal table top

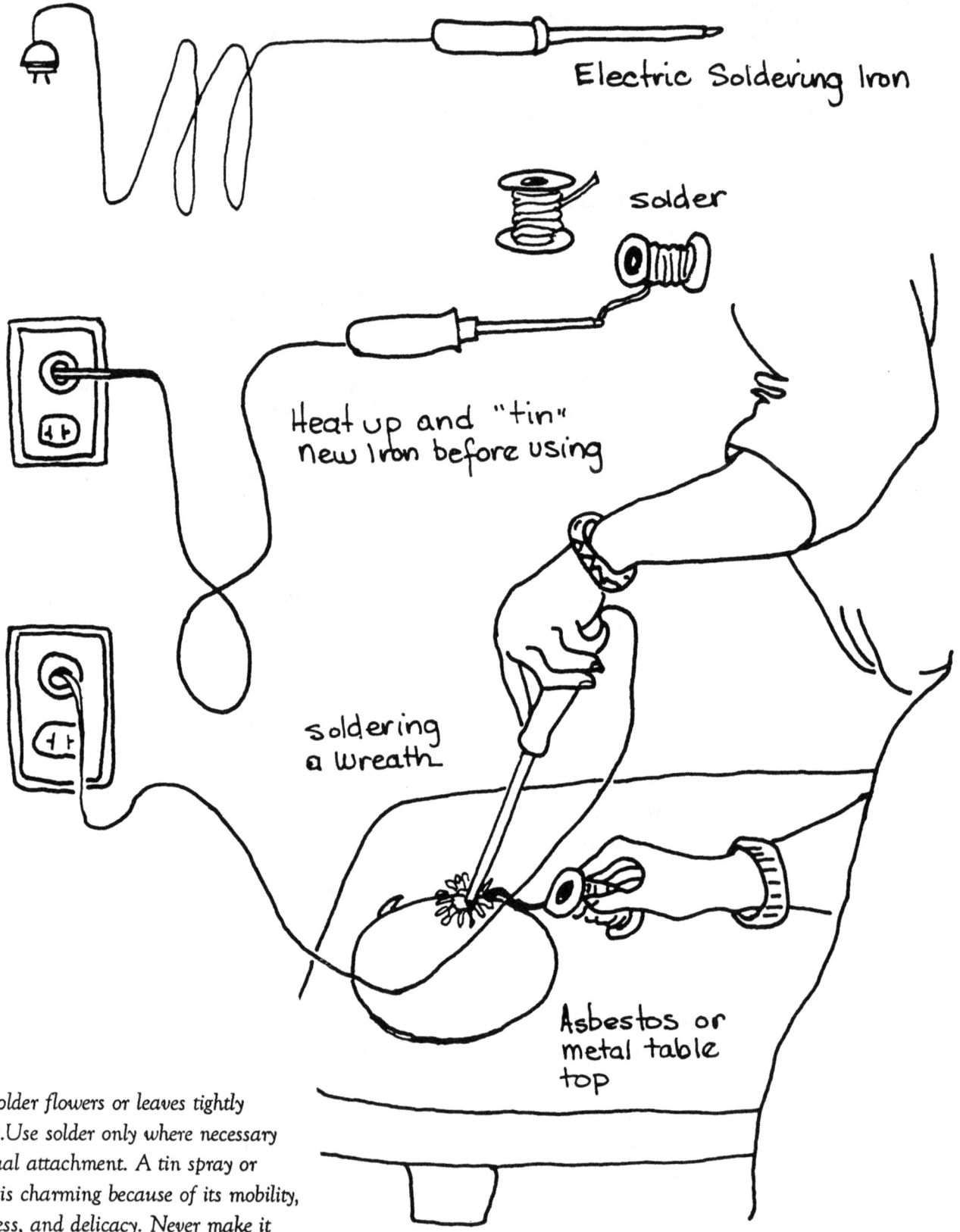

Don't solder flowers or leaves tightly together. Use solder only where necessary for actual attachment. A tin spray or wreath is charming because of its mobility, spinginess, and delicacy. Never make it rigid or stiff.

WHISK
BROOM

SMALL
DUST
PAN

WORKSHOP

Your workshop can be as complete as you wish to make it. If you have a whole room that you can set aside as a tin workshop, you are fortunate. First, you will need shelves to store your tin can collection and walls on which to hang finished pieces, pieces being worked on, and tools. If you plan to sell your work, a wall is the best place to display it. You will also need drawers or boxes to store your jewel collection.

With plenty of space you can have many pieces on hand and in various stages of completion, something almost impossible to do if you are working on the kitchen table or a card table, between time and space that is used for other purposes.

In a large studio that you intend to devote only to tin, you can install a large, strong table to work on. A smaller table in one corner is good to have for making designs away from the cut tin and other materials of actual work, but your large table will hold just about everything else.

If possible, cover your work table with a sheet of Masonite to protect it, and place a sheet of metal or heat resistant pad under the soldering area. On one side lay out all tools for working the tin; on the other side, do the assembly work and the soldering. Coils of wire can hang on nails on the end of the table. Underneath, next to the area where you do your cutting, place a sturdy carton or a large metal waste basket to catch scraps of tin.

On the other hand, if a large studio is not available, you can do tin work beautifully on a small table in one end of the kitchen, living room or in your own bedroom. One young mother who is becoming known all over the country for her beautiful tin work has always worked in her kitchen on a large butcher's block. She has five children, a husband and does all of her housework, and only lately has built her studio in her backyard!

The essential tools and materials, of course, are the same as you would have in a larger space, except that you probably have to be neater, work on one piece at a time, be more considerate of others sharing the room, keep tools and materials put away when not in use, and be more orderly in general.

When sharing a room where the family comes and goes, be especially careful to sweep up scraps of tin every time you finish working. Store extra tin sparingly in drawers or boxes, or even outside in a garage or wherever you can, and bring it in only when needed.

If you plan to sell your tin pieces (and this is one great incentive to spark your work), you can find art and gift shops that will display them and sell them for you at a commission. They may buy them outright. This will eliminate the need to have a display wall at home.

DESIGN AND PATTERN

Using the designs in this book as they are presented will teach you how to use the metal and develop skill and confidence. While you are working on these pieces, you will probably start thinking of how to combine and reorganize the designs in your own ways. Then, you can create entirely new designs. Here you will have to cultivate a "penetrating eye" — that is, you will have to look at things carefully, quietly and thoroughly.

For instance, when Beryl was experimenting with the lily, she discovered that although she was a lifelong gardener with a special love for the day lily, making tin lilies forced her to look at them in a new way.

She examined the lily carefully and cut many flowers apart to find out how they grew. She made sketches and drawings of the various parts, and from this knowledge worked out her tin designs. You can do this with any flower or whatever else you want to make. Whatever your drawing skill, you will learn more if you take the time to plan your design carefully ahead of time.

Designs for tin should be open, simple and not too detailed, and yet there should not usually be great expanses of plain, undecorated tin. A large undecorated surface fails to bring out the delicacy and sparkle desirable in a beautiful piece, while a much detailed piece, too cluttered with tooling or small shapes, loses the reflective quality that makes it attractive.

COLOR

The use of faceted glass costume jewelry, aided by bending, shaping and tooling the metal, results in a truly beautiful article that gives off reflected sparkle and color.

Beryl Boynton, who was something of a purist, made her designs without the use of any added color. She used only the original color of the tin, adding jewels sparingly.

However, after learning the basic procedures and techniques of working the tin, the craftsman should feel free to explore the possibilities of the many and exciting new materials that are put on the market almost daily.

Some that might be suggested are: the many spray paints and metallics; epoxy paint (especially good on metals); the soft, fired-on colored enamels made especially for aluminum and tin; sealing wax and plating.

Always remember that tin craft, like any other art or craft, requires for its best expression a spirited, lively design and an understanding of what the material will and won't do — all of this comes from the experience, imagination, enthusiasm and persistence of the worker. Give it your best!

TIPS AND GUIDELINES:

• A double line inside the edges of a pattern indicates tooling. A single line is to be cut.

• Trace patterns onto cardboard. This makes a sturdy, practical pattern for getting your design onto the tin. Draw around the cardboard with a pencil or stylus.

• In your workshop: large wastebasket, whisk broom or brush, a heat resistant pad for your workbench, and a bulletin board for project ideas.

• If a tin decoration becomes dusty, wash it in a detergent bath of ammonia and water and then spray it with hot water to rinse it. Dry well. It will be a a lovely as ever.

• If a piece of tin does not clean up in a detergent bath, scour it with glass wax or mild abrasive. Jeweler's rouge will remove small spots of rust. First clean the spot thoroughly with steel wool, then put rouge on a soft cloth or piece of felt and polish a small area at a time. Spray immediately with clear plastic. To keep rust from forming and to preserve the brilliance of the tin, spray with a clear lacquer or plastic upon finishing a piece.

IMPORTANT SAFETY MEASURES

• Watch small children and pets in your workroom. Small bits of tin are dangerous if picked up and chewed or swallowed by a child or a puppy. It is almost impossible to keep pieces from falling into their reach.

• Cut tin is sharp and tough; treat it with respect to avoid wounds. Sandpapering will dull a sharp edge. Clip off sharp points.

• Wash hands often when using solder. Acid will eat into hands and clothes.

• Do as little tool work on tin pieces as possible in order to keep the bright, unblemished surface. Any unnecessary scratches or hammering will mar the very thin coating of tin and spoil the appearance of the work.

• Tin must, of course, be kept dry. Don't hang it in a damp place. If it gets wet, be careful to dry it by removing it to a warm place. It is almost sure to rust if it should get wet.

SOME IDEAS FOR USING TIN DECORATIONS

• Combine wreaths of greenery with large gold and silver tin leaves for the holidays — or make a large tin wreath with greenery tied in for color.
• Make a shadowbox to hold a tin wreath or spray. Paint inside of box with a bright color to reflect on the burnished tin. A piece of velvet or felt behind the tin is an effective background.
• Brighten up a dark entrance or hallway. Combine a tin frame with a ceramic figure or plaque.
• Try tin mobiles for a sunny spot, indoors or out.
• Decorative tin motifs set between sheets of plastic make lovely screens, murals, wall-dividers.
• Tin decorations hung on a wall in the patio or garden and allowed to age make nostalgic conversation pieces.
• The tin wreath can be used over a mantel, in a wall niche, over a door, or as a table centerpiece.
• Use the angel at the center of two ribbon swags held on each end by Christmas birds. Hang Christmas cards on the ribbons. This is very effective over a mantel or on a white wall.

Project No. 1 : TWO TIN FRAMES

RECTANGULAR FRAME

Materials: One piece of silver or gold tin 5" x 5½"
               (Cut out carefully to avoid leaving sharp splinters)
               A short piece of wire for a hanging loop

- Measure silver ½" in from edge all around. Mark with pencil or sharp stylus and tool line from front side.
- Measure another ³⁄₁₆" in from last line. Mark and tool in exactly the same way.
- Now with dull tooling awl, indent "dots" all around between two tooled lines,
       working this time from back. Make dots ¼" apart.
- Tool diagonally from outside corner in to corners of dotted decoration, working from front side.
- Turn over and tool marks about ⁵⁄₁₆" apart all around frame.
- Solder wire loop in center of back for hanging frame.
- Smooth the edges with file or sandpaper. Wash thoroughly and dry.
- Paste picture in frame.

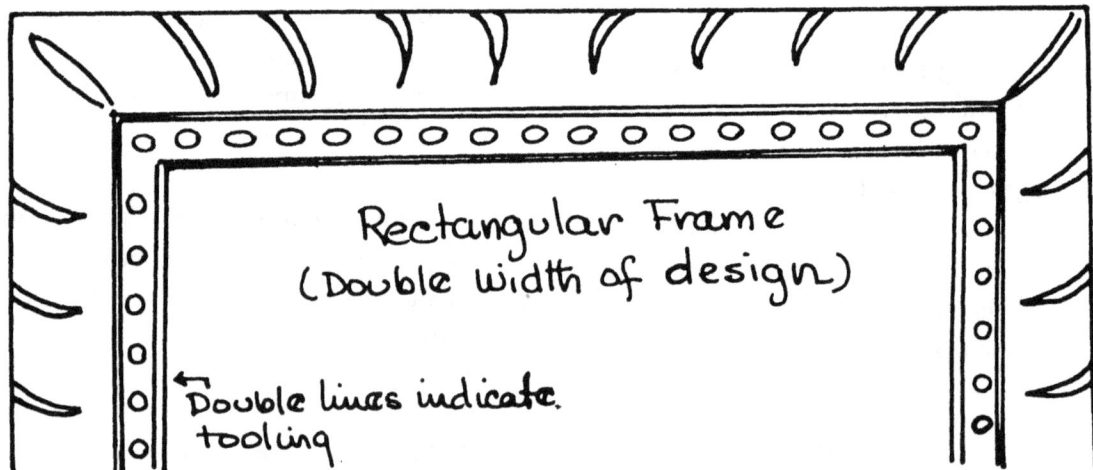

Rectangular Frame
(Double width of design)

Double lines indicate
tooling

Note: For more intricate designs, use leather stamps. Repeat stamp for border designs.

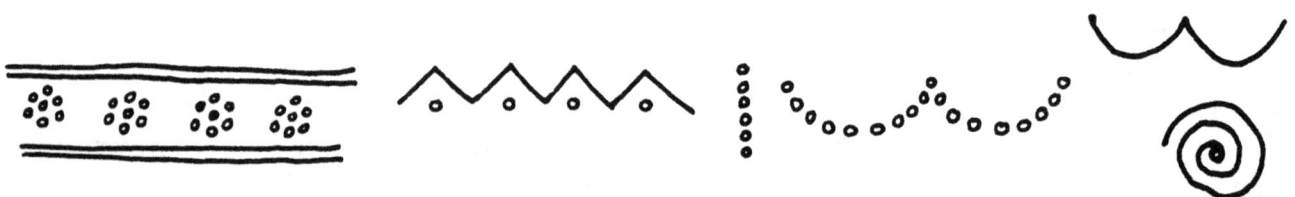

OBLONG FRAME

Double line indicates tooling

←

OBLONG CENTER, PETAL-EDGE FRAME

Materials:
One piece of silver or gold tin 6¾" x 7½"
(Cut out carefully to avoid leaving sharp splinters)
A short piece of wire for a hanging loop

FOLD PATTERN

FOLD PATTERN

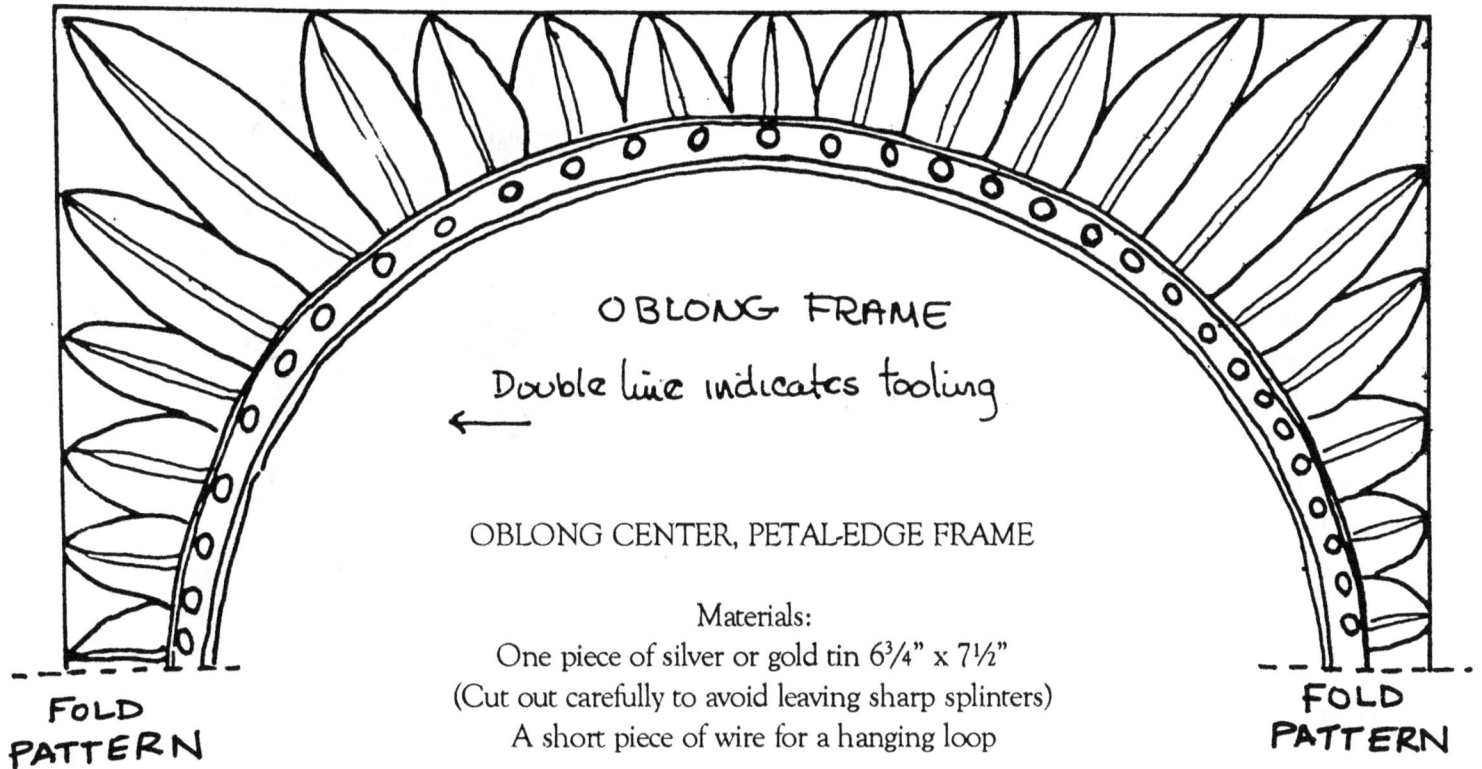

- Using tracing paper same size as tin, lay over frame outline (this page) and draw design.
- Double paper over and draw second half to make complete design.
- Trace onto tin, using carbon paper. Cut out petals. Do not cut center out.
- Make dot decoration with round-pointed awl from back, ¼" apart.
- Tool line in center of each petal from back. This causes petals to curve nicely toward the front.
- Clip all points to round slightly.
- Sandpaper edges. Solder hanging-wire in center of top back.
- Wash. Paste picture inside frame.
- To preserve: wax, or spray with clear plastic.

Project No. 2: FLOWER SPRAY

Materials:

1 stem, 16" long, cut from 16 gauge galvanized wire

4 stems, 5" long, cut from 18 gauge wire

14 cans lids as follows:

2 gold-colored lids, 4" across	5 silver-colored lids, 3" across
2 gold-colored lids, 2½" across	1 silver-colored lid, 2½" across
2 silver-colored lids, 2" across	

Enough silver-colored tin to make five leaves and four strips, each 2½" x ¾"

FLOWER NO. 1:

Lids:

   1 - 4" gold
   1- 3" silver
   1 - 2" silver

- Cut 4" lid in to within ½" of center eight times.
- Clip corners. Cut 3" lid same way, then fringe.
- Cut 2" lid same way except to cut out only four corners. Fringe. Punch two holes in each lid.
- Assemble on wire. Make two flowers like this, but on second flower, snip edges of petals to measure 3½" across to make a smaller flower [1A].

Flower No. 1

Flower No. 2

Flower No. 3

Flower No. 1A

Flower No. 2

FLOWER NO. 2:

Lids:

   1- 3" silver
   1 - 2½" gold
   1 strip, silver

- Cut 3" lid same as 3" flower in No. 1.
- Cut corners out of 2½" lid, and fringe.
- Fringe ends of strip and curl with pliers.
- Punch holes in each piece.
- Assemble on wire.
- Make two of these, same size.

FLOWER SPRAY shown in asymetrical arrangement with large leaves.

FLOWER NO. 3:

Lids:

   1- 3" silver
   1 - 2½" silver
   1 strip, silver

- Make same as Flower No. 2, except all silver.

CUT
PIE SHAPES
OUT —
THEN
FRINGE

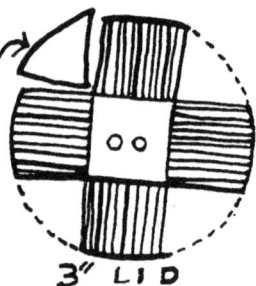

3" LID

MAKE
2½" LID
SAME
AS
3" LID

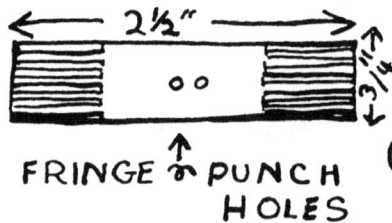

2½"

FRINGE ↑ PUNCH
HOLES

~ FLOWER NO. 2 ~

SAME AS
NO. 1

CURL WITH
PLIERS

LEAVES:

- Use one large silver-colored can, or enough silver tin from several cans to make five of the large leaves.
- Using tracing and carbon papers, transfer pattern onto cardboard and cut out. Then place cardboard pattern on tin.
- Draw around strongly with sharp stylus (a needle or nail will do), and cut out.
- Sandpaper all around to dull edges.
- Make five leaves.
- Fringe as shown in diagram.
- **Variation:** Instead of large leaves, make the small pointed leaves shown at right, two together, and twist around stems. Make twelve pairs of leaves.

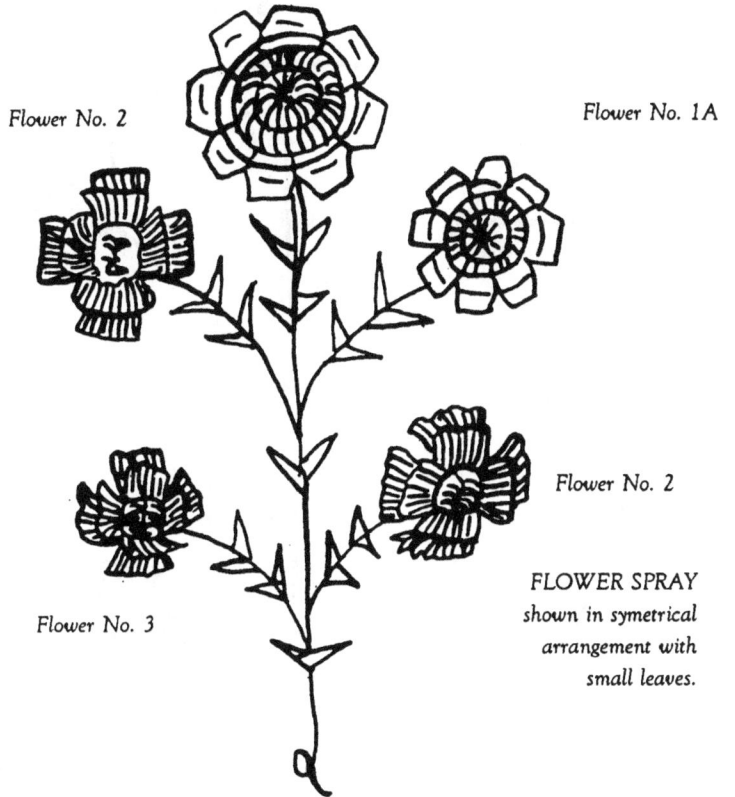

TO ASSEMBLE AND COMPLETE SPRAY:

- Attach flowers to stems with wires, wrapping and twisting securely.
- Keep all attachments behind spray.
- Wire short stems onto main stem.
- Wrap long ends of leaves around stems, or punch holes and attach with wires. If you wish, you can later solder all joints together, being careful to keep solder on back as much as possible.
- Tie or solder wire loop to center in back for hanging.
- When all flowers and leaves have been attached, examine to see if there is anything you have forgotten. Then arrange and bend flowers and leaves into natural positions.
- If you have used solder, wash the piece in hot detergent bath and spray with clean, hot water to rinse.
- Let it dry, and then hang up your first lovely tin flower piece!

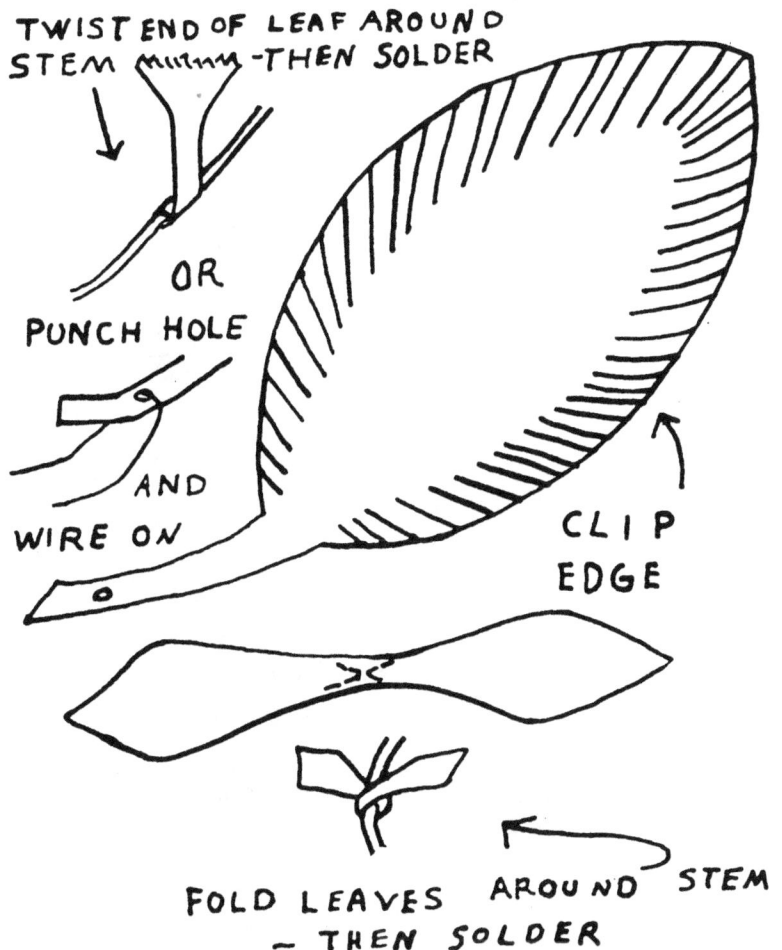

NOTE: Measure and count at first, but try to learn to work spontaneously. Your flowers will be more natural looking and you will enjoy it more!

Flower No. 1

Flower No. 2

Flower No. 1A

Flower No. 2

Flower No. 3

FLOWER SPRAY
*shown in symetrical
arrangement with
small leaves.*

TWIST END OF LEAF AROUND STEM — THEN SOLDER

OR

PUNCH HOLE

AND

WIRE ON

CLIP EDGE

FOLD LEAVES AROUND STEM — THEN SOLDER

4" GOLD LID, EXACT SIZE

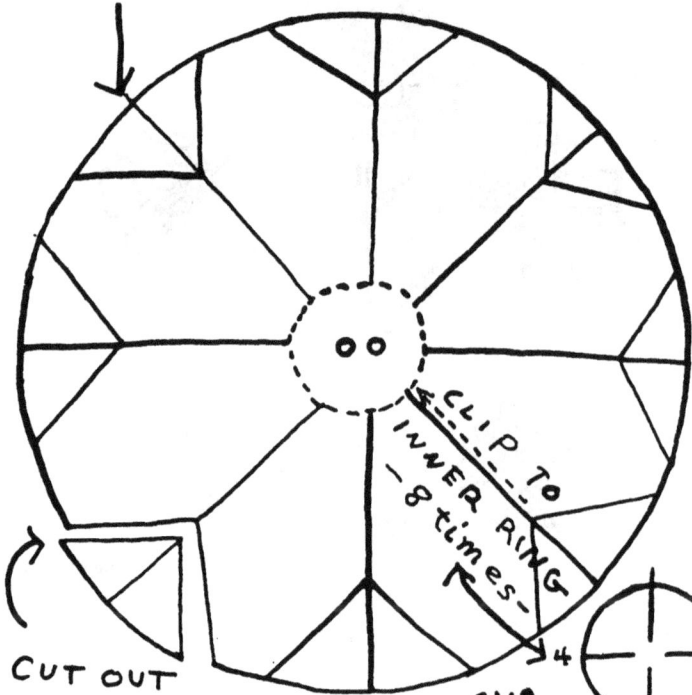

CLIP TO INNER RING — 8 times —

CUT OUT PIE-SHAPED CORNERS, THEN FRINGE PETALS

CLIP 8 TIMES

4 ← → 1
8 3 5
7 6

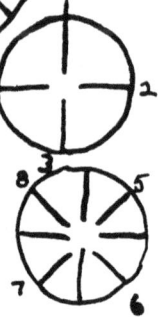

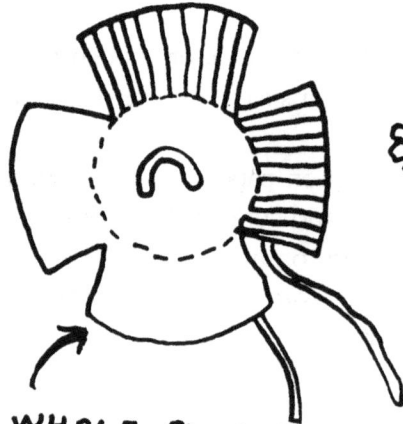

WHOLE FLOWER ASSEMBLED BUT NOT PULLED TOGETHER

NO. 1 FLOWER ASSEMBLED AND SHAPED ON WIRE.

SIDE VIEW OF FLOWER, WIRED AND ATTACHED TO STEM.

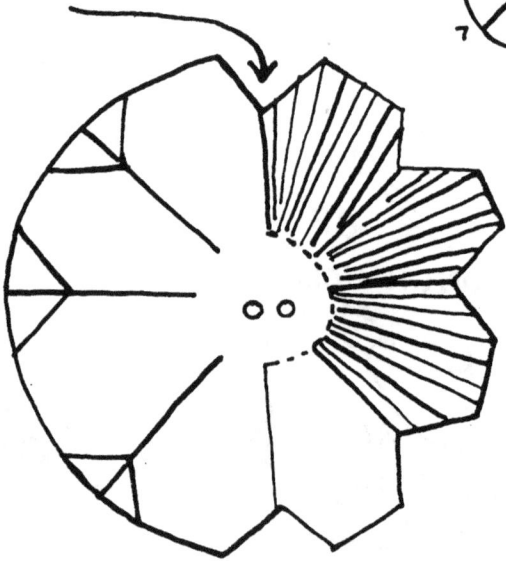

USE A THICK MAGAZINE TO WORK ON — NICE AND SPRINGY!

MAKE HOLES WITH HAMMER AND SMALL NAIL.

Project No. 3: WREATH

MAKE 2 OF THESE FLOWERS AND YOU WILL HAVE THE TOP AND BOTTOM FLOWERS OF THE WREATH.

Materials:

For two large flowers:
  2 - 4" gold lids
  2 - 3" silver lids
  2 gold or silver strips - 1" wide and 3" long
  2 clusters of brilliant jewels

For ten small flowers:
  10 - 3" gold lids
  10 - 2½" silver lids
  10 gold or silver strips - 1" wide and 2½" long

For leaves:
  1 flattened gold-colored can with ends and seams
      removed

For wreath shape and stems:
  24 inches of No. 22 gauge wire
  36 inches of No. 16 gauge wire

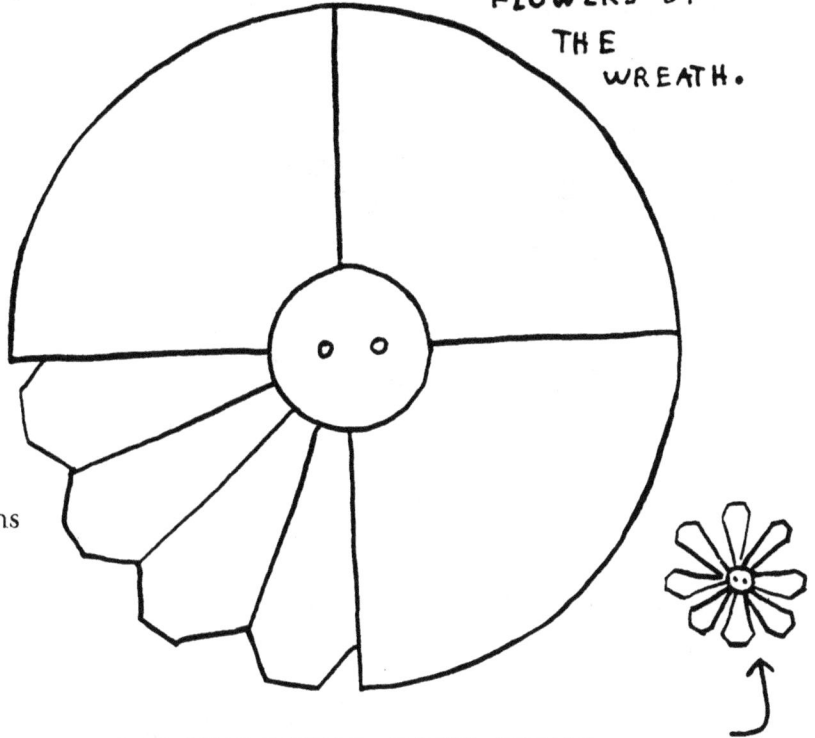

Tools:

small hammer	awl
poultry shears or tin snips	soldering iron
pliers	acid core solder

LARGE FLOWERS - OUTER PETALS:

- Draw a 1" circle in center of lid if there is not one pressed in.
- Cut down to circle on four sides.
- Make three extra cuts to circle in each quarter as shown in sketch.
- Snip corners off petals.
- Bend up from circle.
- Punch two holes.

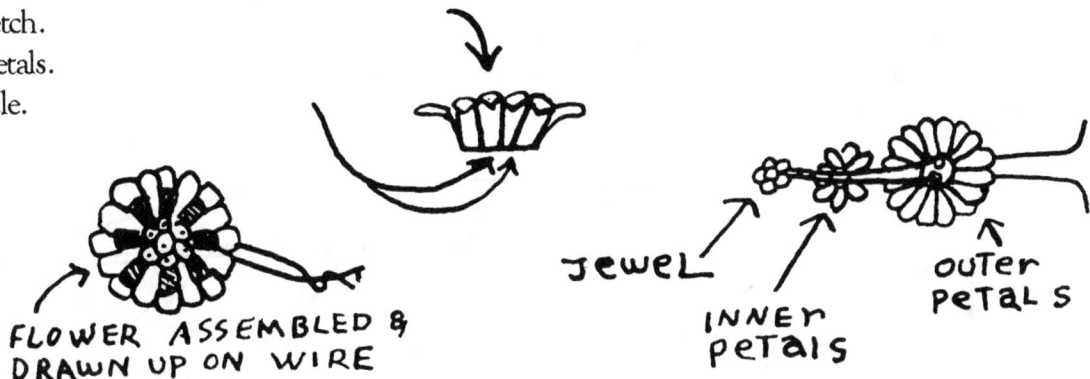

LARGE FLOWERS - INNER PETALS:

- Using 3" silver lid, repeat as for outer petal to step 4.
- Cut out and discard every other petal.
- Bend up. Punch holes.
- Put jewels and petals on small wire, twist to hold, and lay aside to solder, later.

FLOWER ASSEMBLED & DRAWN UP ON WIRE

JEWEL

INNER PETALS

OUTER PETALS

TEN SMALL FLOWERS FOR SIDES OF WREATH:

• Using 3" gold lids (outer petals) and 2½" silver lids (inner petals), cut pie shapes out of each corner and clip fringe as shown.

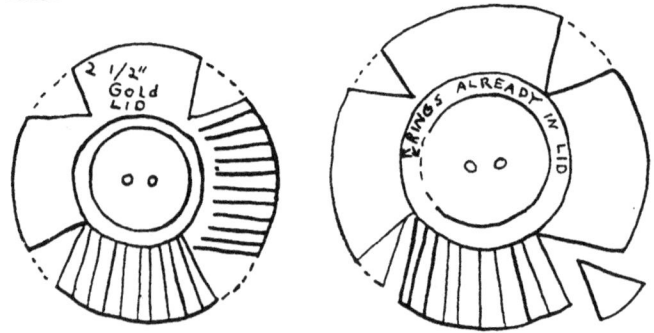

• Using one gold or silver strip for each flower center, clip fringe, punch and curl as shown.
• Assemble pieces on wire and lay aside to solder later.
• Repeat process for each of the remaining flowers.

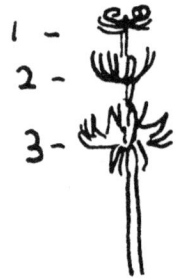

TO ASSEMBLE THE WREATH AND MAKE THE LEAVES:

OVERLAP→ (TWIST TIGHTLY)

TOP & BOTTOM FLOWERS WIRED IN PLACE

• Take the 36" length of 16 gauge wire and bend to make a circle or hoop. Overlap the ends and twist them together.

• Make the hoop into a perfect oval, and, by twisting the wires used to assemble the parts of the flowers, attach one of the large flowers with jeweled center top, and the other to the bottom of the hoop.

• Lay the hoop and the two attached flowers down on the table, flowers facing down. Now space the smaller flowers evenly, five on each side, and twist the wires as securely as you can around the hoop wire. Turn it over carefully and adjust spacing.

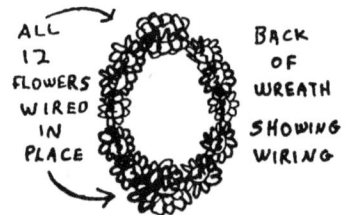

ALL 12 FLOWERS WIRED IN PLACE

BACK OF WREATH SHOWING WIRING

• Trace leaf pattern (below) and transfer with carbon paper to cardboard.
• Cut out cardboard pattern. Draw around pattern with stylus, nail or other sharp point, to trace eight leaves on the flat sheet of tin from the side of a can.

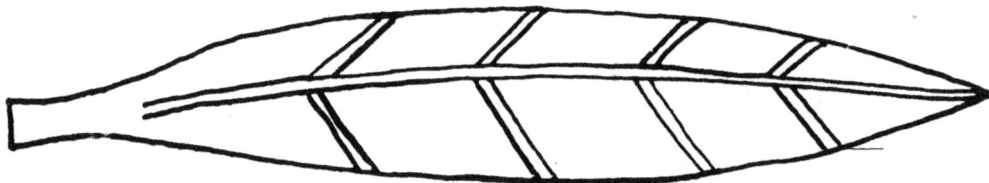

Tooling the leaves:

- Lay a leaf on a thick paper (magazine, catalog, etc.), and, using your dull, cold chisel and hammer, tool from back along veining. The chisel will slide along as it is struck by the hammer, making a continuous even line. If the cold chisel is a little hard to manage, try a dull heavy knife and work it on scrap pieces until you acquire the skill you need. Hold edge of knife or chisel in place and strike continuously as you move along.

TOOLING →

- Attach leaf to hoop temporarily by rolling end around wire between flowers.

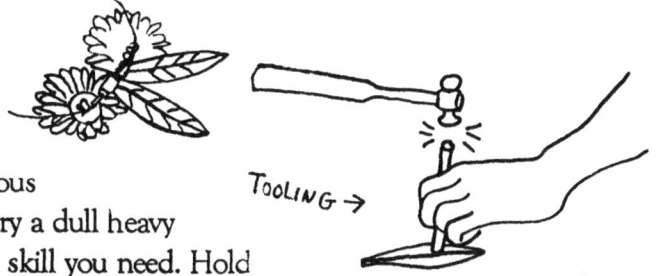

Soldering:

- When flowers are well-spaced and attached with the twisted wires from each unit, lay wreath face down on work table and plug in your soldering iron. Have the spool of acid core solder ready. Place the tip of iron on spot to be soldered; let it heat the tin. It helps to have the area warm. Touch the solder on the iron, and as soon as it melts a little, place on the spot and let it run to the joint. The parts to be soldered must be held steady and tightly together until solder cools (a second or two). Solder all the flowers and leaves onto hoop. As soon as the piece is finished, wash in hot detergent water in sink or bathtub. Scrub with long-handled brush. Rinse, shake water off, and dry in sun or other warm place.

JEWEL FOR EYE.

PATTERN FOR BIRD

— TOOL ALL INSIDE DESIGN, WORKING FROM BACK — USE ROUND METAL PIPE AND COLD CHISEL OR BACK OF HEAVY KNIFE.

- Never solder flowers or leaves tightly together. Use solder only where necessary for actual attachment. A tin spray or wreath is charming for its mobility, springiness and delicacy. Never make it rigid or stiff.

- The addition of a bird, as shown in photograph, enhances the wreath. Cut bird from tracing in the same way the leaves were cut, using pattern on this page. Attach to wreath in the same way as leaves, between flowers, by twisting sharp end around hoop wire, then soldering it on. Use a pretty pin or earring jewel for the eye, attaching it with wire put through hole and soldered on back.

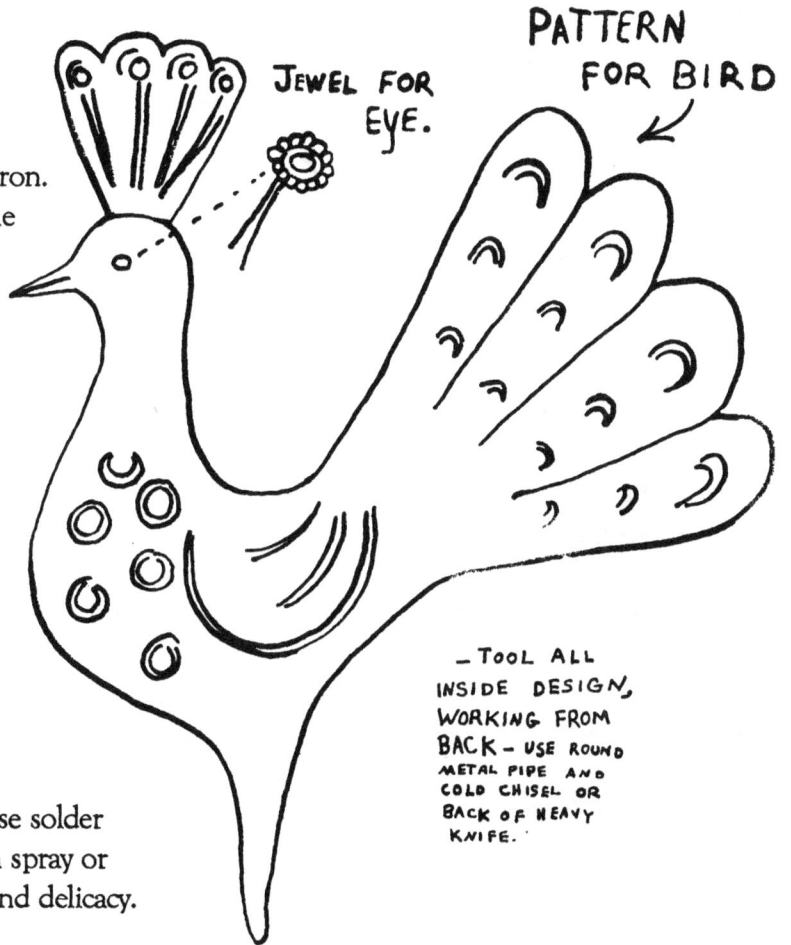

NOTE: For variation, with the same flowers and same length of wire as for a wreath, make a flat spray for a centerpiece or other decoration.

Project No. 4: SPRAY OF LILIES

Materials:

Enough gold-colored tin for nine lily pattern shapes
and nine strips of 3" x ½" for lily stamens
9 stems, 4" long, cut from 16 gauge wire
Enough gold-colored tin for five bud pattern shapes
5 stems, 4" long, cut from 16 gauge wire
10" length of 16 gauge wire

LILY FLOWERS:

- Make cardboard template from pattern. Cut out and
  trace on tin using stylus. Cut out nine pieces.
- Tool down center of each petal on double line,
  using blunt knife blade or cold chisel.
- Tool dots with blunt nail or awl. Work from back.
- Bend and shape flowers with pliers and fingers.
  Where petals converge, grip with pliers and pull
  into tiny circle, then bend petals realistically
  out and back.

LILY STAMENS:

- Snip each of the nine strips 5 or 6 times leaving
  one end attached.
- Fold or roll around nose of pliers and curl ends.
- Make a loop in one end of 4" long wire an push
  down through stamen cluster. Pull down
  tightly and secure with pliers.
- Draw whole stamen cluster down through
  bottom of flower. Solder. Complete each
  flower this way.

BUDS:

- Cut five lily buds from pattern. Clip on dotted
  line. Tool in same way as lily. Bend around
  pliers. Bend petals together at top.
- Pull 4" long wire through each bud in same way
  as lily. Solder

ASSEMBLY OF SPRAY:

- Wrap and twist wires of three buds around one end of the 10" length of wire. Solder.
- Wrap remaining buds onto other end. Solder in place. Insert flowers one at a time into design. Twist and
  weave in and around main stem wire, then solder, coming toward center. Work first one end, then the
  other. This allows solder to cool on one end while you work on the other. Wash your hands often.

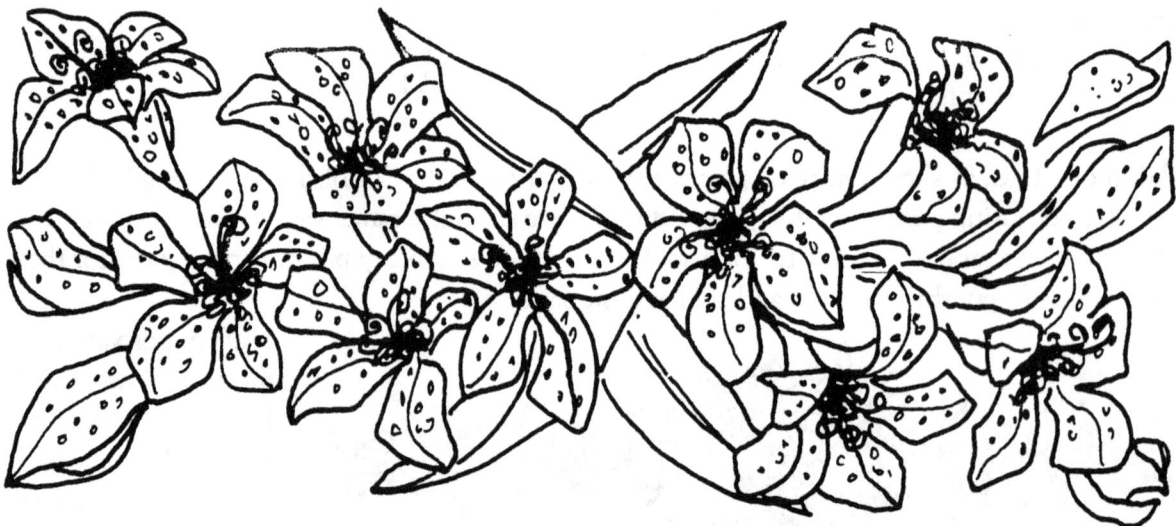

Cut 9 of these

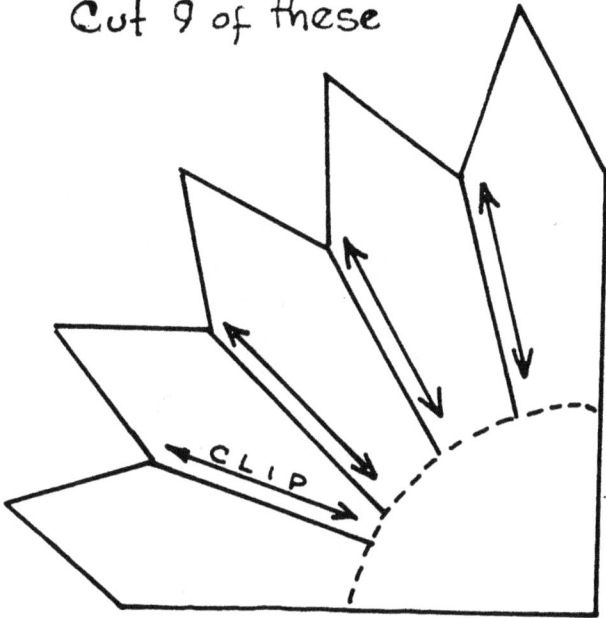

CLIP

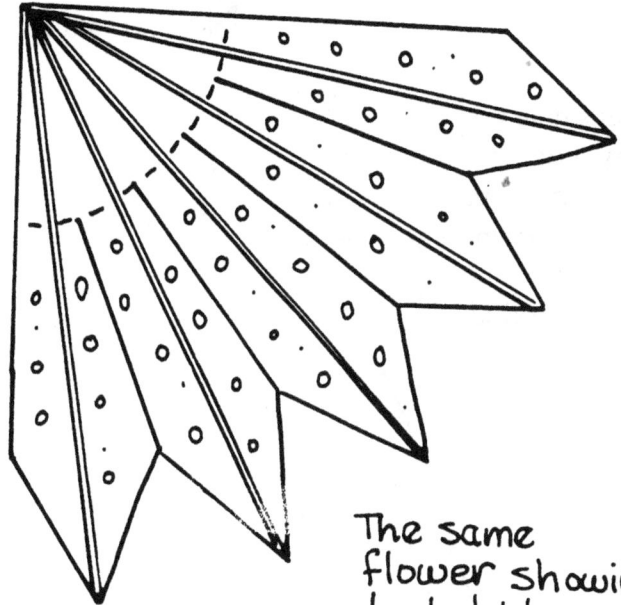

The same flower showing tooled lily spots

Lily bud

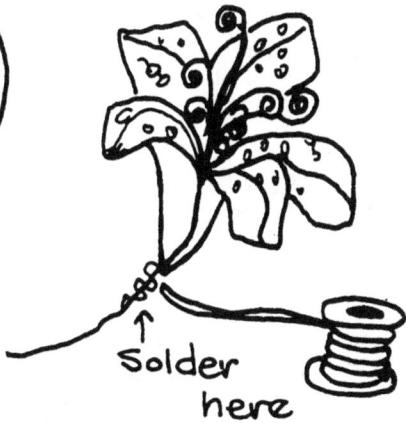

Solder here

Pliers

silver stamens

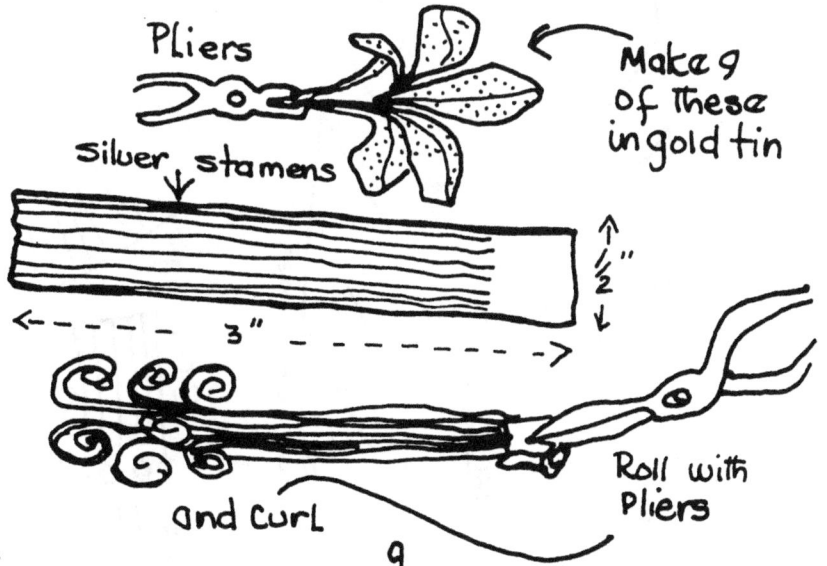

Make 9 of these in gold tin

½"

3"

and curl

Roll with Pliers

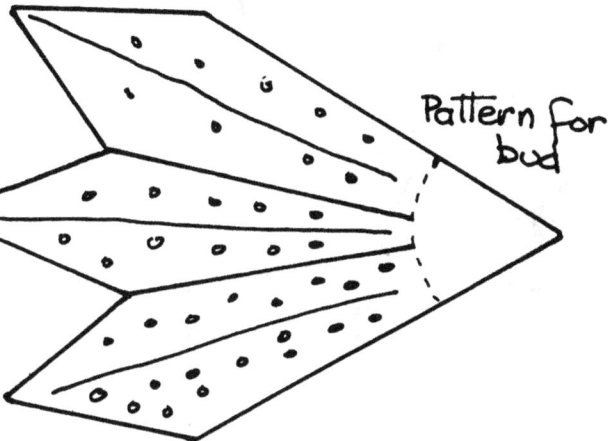

Pattern for bud

Project No. 5: THE JEWELLED ORCHID

By this time you might like
to try your hand at designing
a decorative spray, cluster or
single ornament of your own.
See what you can do
with this orchid.

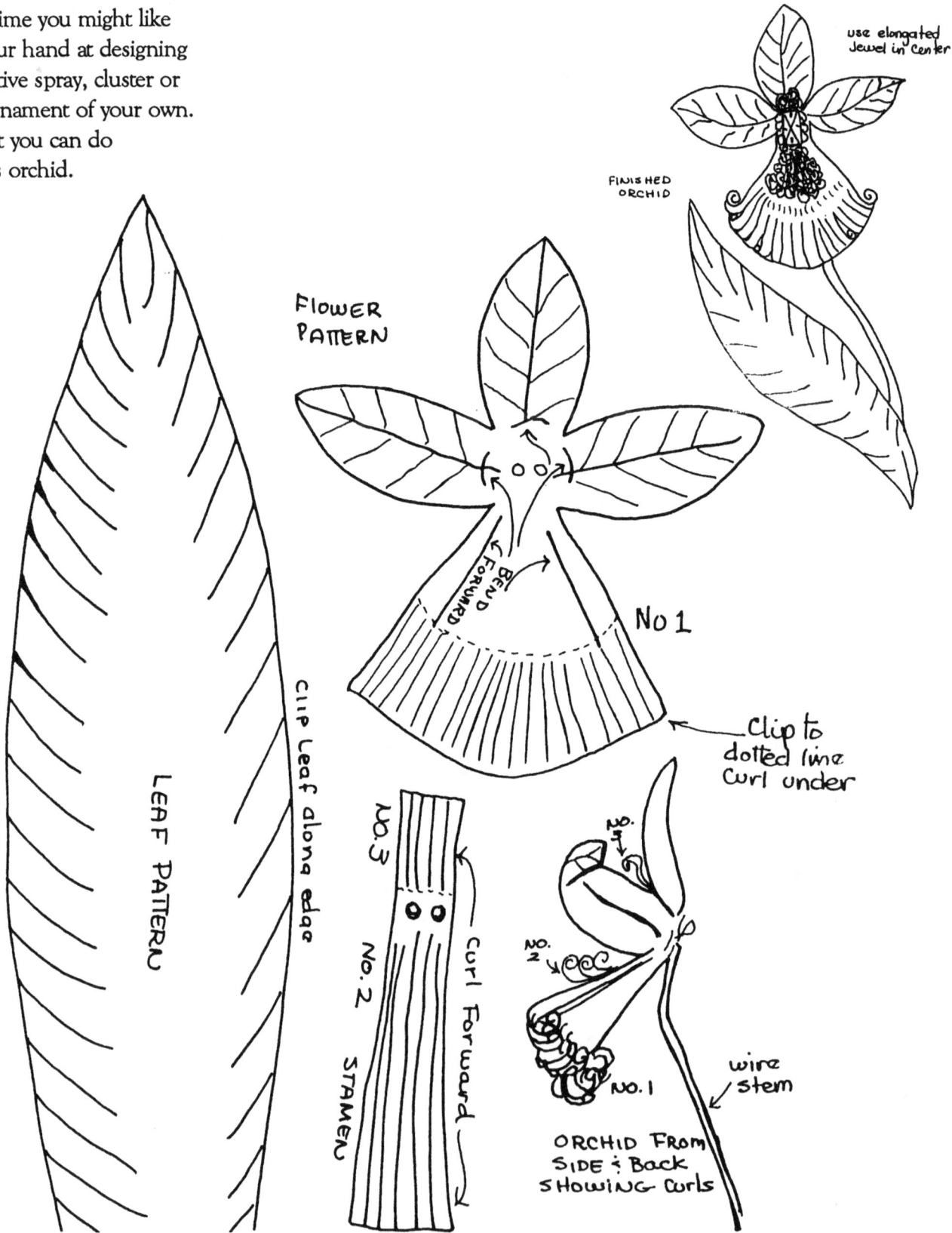

use elongated
jewel in center

FINISHED
ORCHID

FLOWER
PATTERN

BEND FORWARD

No 1

Clip to
dotted line
curl under

LEAF PATTERN

Clip leaf along edge

NO. 3

NO. 2 STAMEN

Curl Forward

NO. 4

NO. 2

NO. 1

wire
stem

ORCHID FROM
SIDE & BACK
SHOWING CURLS

Project No. 6: LARGE DAISY SPRAY

This daisy spray is one of the loveliest and most decorative of any project made with tin. Its delicate, fragile quality depends largely on the skillful cutting of the pieces.

Materials:

16 gauge wire: 1 piece - 21" long
                2 pieces, 17" long
                2 pieces 12" long
Enough tin to cut out all the pattern pieces

FLOWERS:

- Assemble petals into groups for the five flowers. Four large and four small petals make each flower (or two sets of double petals as shown in pattern). Cutting two petals together makes it easier to assemble and solder.
- Choose small clusters of colored glass for centers. Using small wire, tie petals together and onto stem wires. Tie the jewels in place, shaping and arranging petals before soldering.

LEAVES:

- Assemble and attach five large leaves (No. 1) on center stem wire. One large leaf at bottom of each of the other four stems. All other leaves are small (No. 2).
- After all stems are complete and soldered securely, arrange stems to form flat spray. Wrap small wire around lower four inches of stems, tying them firmly together.
- To hang the spray on the wall, make a small loop just behind the tallest leaf.
- When all sprays are bound together, arrange on back of base leaf cluster and solder.

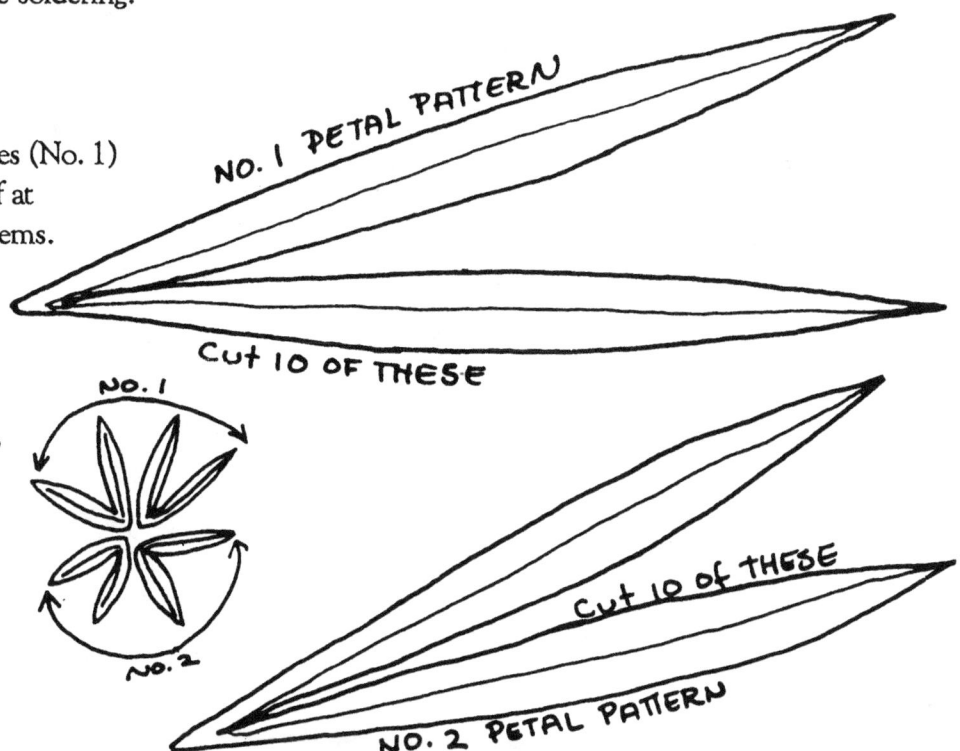

DAISY SPRAY

NO. 1 PETAL PATTERN

CUT 10 OF THESE

NO. 1

NO. 2

CUT 10 OF THESE

NO. 2 PETAL PATTERN

TINCRAFT
28

Back,
Showing
Solder

Fold Leaves
Around stem.
Spot solder
to back.

BASE CLUSTER
PATTERN

(Tool on BACK)

LEAF PATTERN
cut 9

1

LEAF PATTERN

2   cut 16

Project No. 7: ANGEL

This festive piece can be made as a hanging decoration or to stand on its own.

Materials:

Enough gold-colored tin for wings, sash and sleeves
Enough silver-colored tin for angel's body and arms
    (Use two cans, each 4" high and 12" around)
- For hanging version: 6" length of wire for loop
- For standing version: 7½" x ¾" strip of tin for stand

- Using patterns, cut out pieces from appropriate
    colored tin, and clip as shown.
- Tool eyes, mouth and hair from back.
- Place arms under sleeves to dotted line,
    then solder.
- Place sash at "x" (see next page)
    on angel's body, then solder.
- Place sleeves and arms in position on body.
    Solder behind shoulders.
- Place wings in position and solder.
- Curl crown and ends of sash forward.

For hanging Angel:
- Loop 6" wire around base of wings and
    up behind head and twist together.

For standing Angel:
- Solder one end of ¾" strip directly
    in back of hands. Bend
    bottom of strip out 1".

FINISHED ANGEL

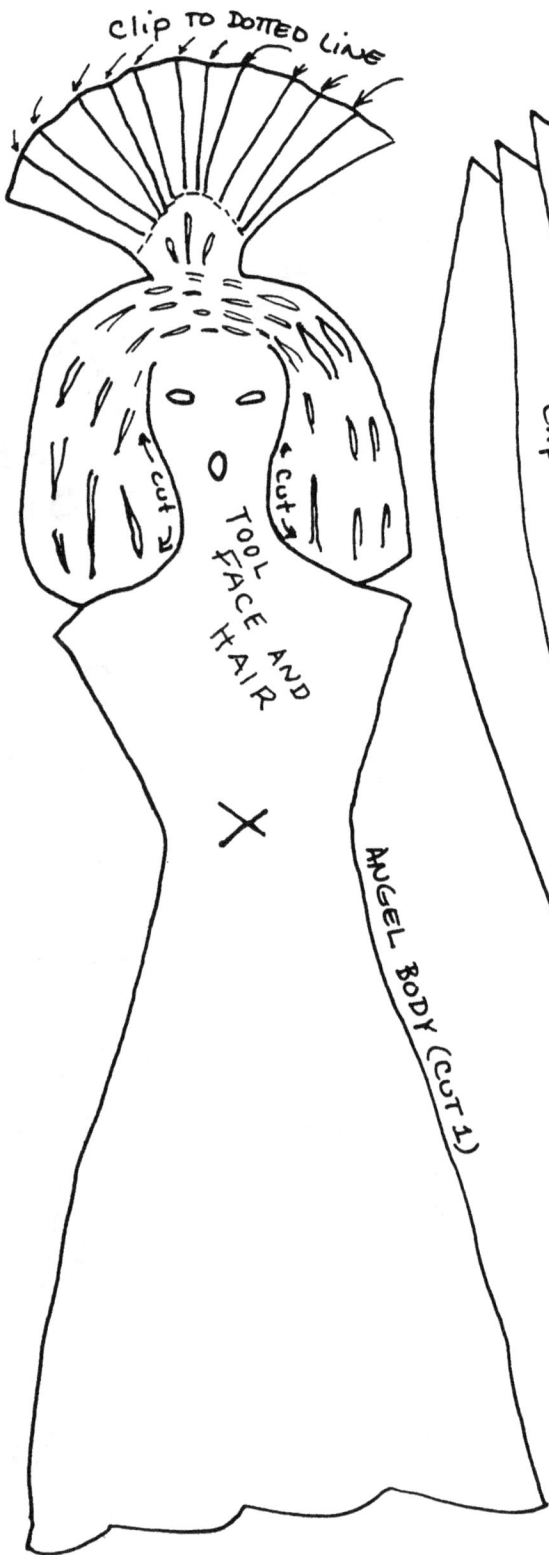

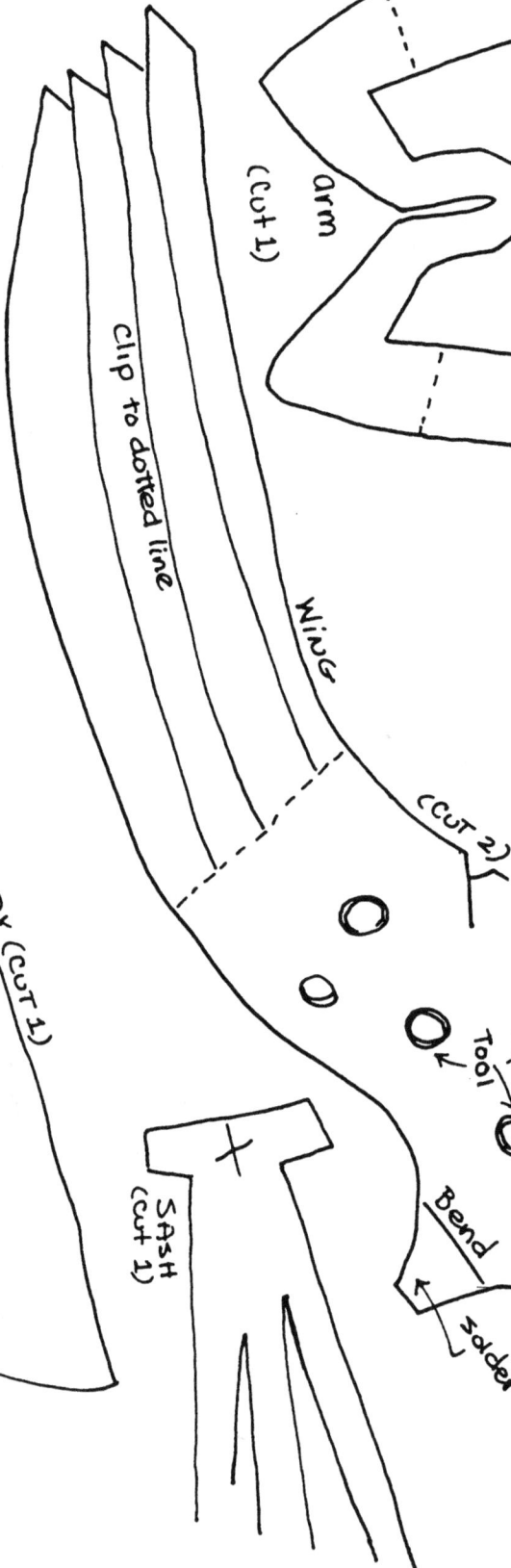

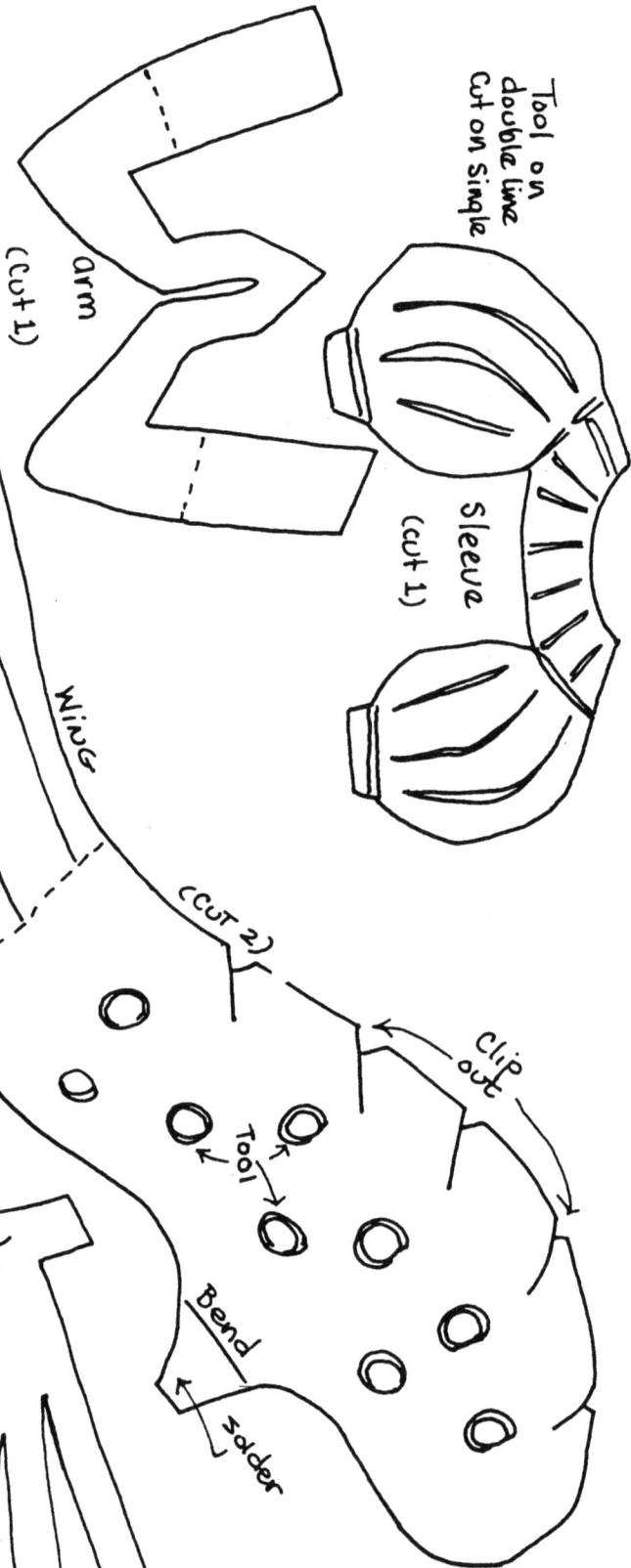

CLIP TO DOTTED LINE

Tool on double line
Cut on single

arm
(cut 1)

Sleeve
(cut 1)

TOOL AND FACE AND HAIR

cut

cut

Clip to dotted line

Wing

(cut 2)

Clip out

Tool

Bend

Solder

ANGEL BODY (cut 1)

SASH
(cut 1)

Project No. 8: CHRISTMAS BIRD

This lively Christmas bird made be used as a single ornament
or in pairs to hold a holiday swag for Christmas cards and light Christmas balls.

Materials:

Use your favorite colors of tin to cut out the pattern pieces of each bird as shown
Cut a strip of tin 1" wide and 9" long, snipped and curled as shown — one for each bird
Jewels for eyes

NO.1

USE 2 BIRDS and a LINE MADE OF CHRISTMAS
RIBBON TO DISPLAY HOLIDAY CARDS.

NO.2 DECORATION FOR MANTEL,
DOOR OR WALL.

HANGING WIRE   SOLDER TIN COILS ON
BACK OF BEAK

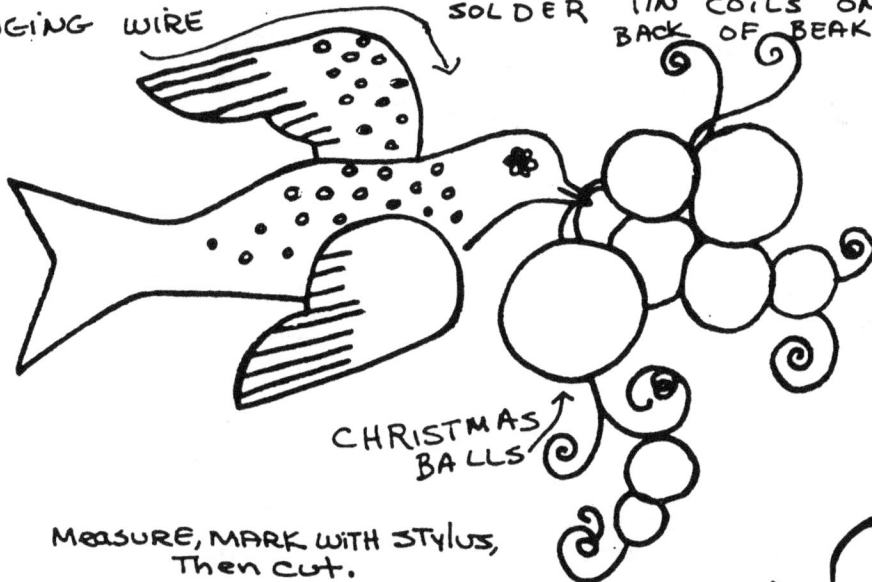

CHRISTMAS
BALLS

MEASURE, MARK WITH STYLUS,
THEN CUT.

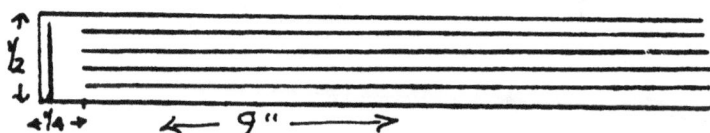

1"   9"

TOOL HALF
CIRCLES

A
SWAG
MADE
OF CHRISTMAS
GREENS

Jewel eye
(attach w/ wire
Through punched
hole. Solder on back.)

(use metal Rod
or pipe)
Work from
back

GOLD
BODY_
SILVER
WINGS _ OR
REVERSE

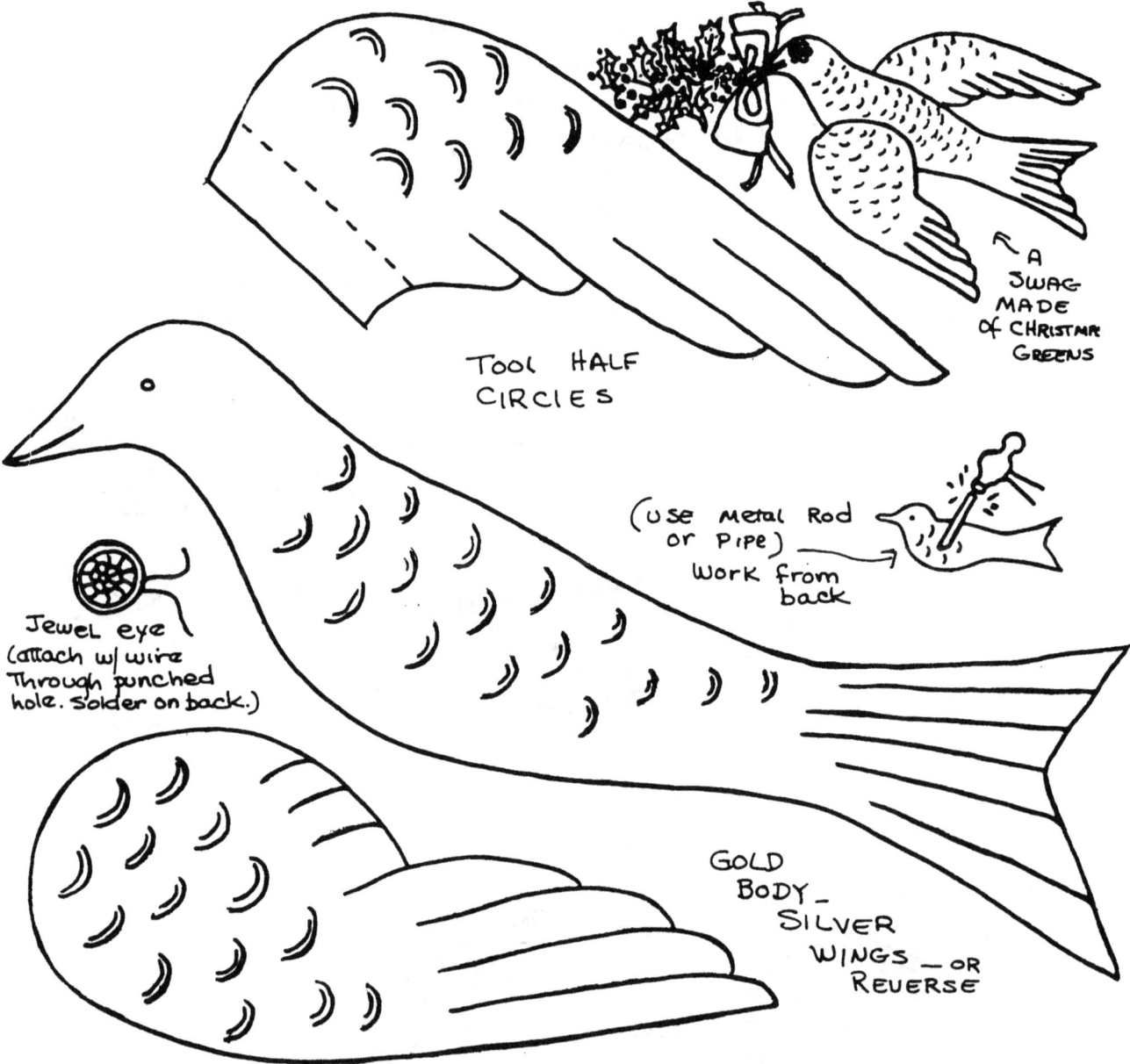

SOLDER WIRE
ON BACK TO HANG UP BY

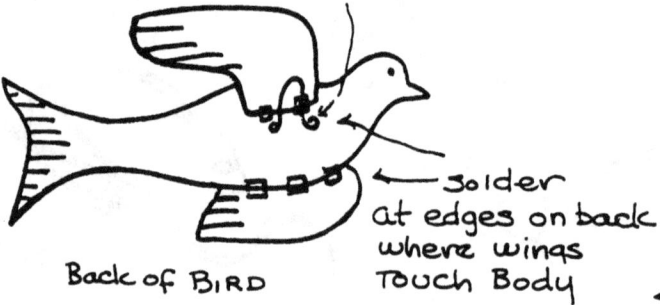

Back of Bird

Solder
at edges on back
where wings
Touch Body

(Place wings carefully---
TURN OVER TO SOLDER)

www.ingramcontent.com/pod-product-compliance
Lightning Source LLC
Chambersburg PA
CBHW062115090426
42741CB00016B/3428